CallCenterToday.com

How to Become a GREAT
Call Center Manager

Strategies and Solutions for the People in your Call Center – Supervisors, Trainers, Managers, Executives and Agents

Dan Coen

Senior Book Editor: Howard Cole

CallCenterToday.com.

The human engineering of call centers and people.
Solutions for managers, executives, trainers, and team leaders.

What Others Say About
CallCenterToday.com and Dan Coen

Several functions need to blend together in order to drive performance in the call center. Technology, messaging, media, and of course, the people. Dan gets it. He strings the processes together.

Joseph C. Volpe
Chief Operating Officer
Integrated Media Solutions

Being good isn't enough when it comes to managing people. Dan teaches call center managers to be great.

Jerry Feldman
President
CallSource

Dan truly understands the human side of managing call center agents. He helped guide our operating foundation and our people.

Ron Miller
Managing Partner
Miller and Associates

I'm writing to thank you for contributing to my success story. Using some of the information in the seminar, my team lead and I developed a team with high morale and high production and landed a very large new account. In turn, I applied for and was offered the position of program manager. WOW, successful people management really does make the difference in the call center.

Shari Shaw
Program Manager
WorldTravel.com

Dan understands the human engineering of call centers. Monitoring calls, listening to tapes, coaching agents, providing feedback. His training on supervising agents provides immediate benefit.

Chuck Hengel
President
Marketing Architects

We have been very pleased to have Dan as a featured speaker for several of our Customer Care Forums. His presentations and workshops on call center development and management have received high ratings from participants. Dan communicates very well with all levels of Customer Care and call center staff – from front line reps and trainers to managers and senior executives.

Roger Nunley
Managing Director
Customer Care Institute

Dan provides definitive management strategies and training programs to the most important part of the call center – the people and its management.

Gary Blasiar
President
Alert Communications

Dan Coen changed the way we understood call center operations. His programs on the human engineering side of performance improved our results immeasurably.

Dan Coffey
Director
Critical Path

Dan has broken the myth that effective telephone sales are unteachable skills.

Jay Check
President
Cape Enterprises

Great books, wonderful marketing strategies, terrific team player. We've worked with Dan, and CallCenterToday.com, on dozens of projects, and our clients agree: 100% outstanding!

Linda Hoffman
Executive Director
Image Advertising

Dan enhanced our entire management philosophy. He impacted our performance and our people.

Howard Goodman
President
Goodman Communications West

How many people do what they say and say what they do? Over and over again, Dan maps out a strategy, designs performance development programs, and delivers. Our management team, our agents, and our bottom line results all benefit from the call center development programs, and processes, that Dan implements.

Ken Nelson
Director of Sales and Marketing
Renaissance Agencies

Dan Coen's message is a wake-up call for call center managers asleep at the touchpad.

Gerhard Gschwandtner
Publisher
Selling Power Magazine

It's important to get the job done. Dan has worked with our organization on training the management team, telephone sales strategy and operations. He's invaluable on bringing projects from inception to completion.

Chuck Ciarlo
President
Left Bank Solutions

Call Center management is all about people and personalizing the message to deliver better results. Dan Coen embraces the culture of the call center and teaches how to do it the right way.

Joie Pitre
Marketing Director
Guthy-Renker

Over the last year I have added only one book to my teleservices library. That book was Dan Coen's <u>Friendly Persuasion</u>.

Tom Cardella
President
Precision Response Corporation

Dan's books, especially Building Call Center Culture, have been instrumental to teaching call center management.

Mitch Ross
Sales Director
Vision X

Dan understands team work, and that is essential to great marketing and management. He has helped put together some terrific projects for us.

Elliot Leiboff
Chief Operating Officer
CallSource

Dan knows call centers. He's helped move PhoneWare to the next level, especially with his strategy on telephone sales, cross selling and bundling. Dan has been a top-notch partner over the years.

Bill Nassir
President
PhoneWare, Inc.

CallCenterToday.com Presents:

How to Become a GREAT Call Center Manager

Strategies and Solutions for the People in your Call Center – Supervisors, Trainers, Managers, Executives and Agents

Dan Coen

Senior Book Editor: Howard Cole

CallCenterToday.com.

The human engineering of call centers and people.
Solutions for managers, executives, trainers, and team leaders.

How to Become a GREAT Call Center Manager

Strategies and Solutions for the People in your Call Center
Supervisors, Trainers, Managers, Executive and Agents

Copyright 2004 by Dan Coen and DCD Publishing First Printing

All Rights Reserved   Printed in USA

DCD Publishing Books may be purchased for educational, business or sales promotion purposes, and are available at a special discount when ordered in bulk. Please contact: Marketing Department, DCD Publishing, P.O. Box 571533, Tarzana, CA 91357. 888-835-5326.
Marketing@CallCenterToday.com

www.CallCenterToday.com or www.DCDPublishing.com

Design by Foglia Publications: 408-970-9562.

Howard Cole, Senior Editor. MrWrte@aol.com.

ISBN: 0-9660436-6-9

This publication is published with the understanding that the publisher and author are not engaged in rendering legal advice.

*To those who strive to perfect
the human engineering of call centers and people.
Managers, trainers, executives,
agents and team leaders.*

TABLE OF CONTENTS

CallCenterToday.com Presents:

How to Become a GREAT Call Center Manager

Strategies and Solutions for the People in your Call Center – Supervisors, Trainers, Managers, Executives and Agents

Dan Coen

CALL CENTER BILL OF RIGHTS

Amendment I

Management shall make no rule prohibiting meetings between management and agents on topics of importance to any party. Management commits to the value of regular open communication amongst employees and staff. Management encourages agents to petition the company for a redress of grievances.

Amendment II

All call center policies and procedures, being necessary to the promotion of a quality call center, must be respected by agents, and shall not be infringed.

Amendment III

No agent shall be asked to perform duties for which they have not been trained on. This call center commits to quality training and organization for all employees.

Amendment IV

This call center encourages open contests, prizes and games. Management will ensure that every team in the call center has the ability to participate in programs that reward them for meeting attainable objectives.

Amendment V

Call Center agents agree that they will perform their duties to the best of their abilities within the course of their scheduled work hours.

Amendment VI

Management guarantees a wonderful work environment, with positive training, meetings and exterior environment that ensures the work environment is a fun place to be.

Amendment VII

In issues of disagreement between agents and supervisors, the right to meet with senior management shall be preserved. Management believes in a quality program to mediate disagreements in a sincere and timely manner.   .

Amendment VIII

Management and agents agree to work together to better the performance of projects. This means that when a project is not meeting its objectives, both parties will convene to better performance. This can be accomplished through training, assessment of fundamentals, etc.

Amendment IX

The enumeration in these Bill of Rights of certain rights shall not be construed to deny or disparage other rights retained by the agents and management.

Amendment X

Management and Agents reserve the right to work together to develop more Bill of Rights, and to amend those Bill of Rights already in place.

* Excerpted from *Building Call Center Culture*, by Dan Coen (DCD Publishing)

Introduction

We, as managers, need to try something fresh each day. Sometimes we coach, sometimes we train. One day we discipline, another we motivate. Often we just plain listen. Constantly, we are required to drive results.

"How to Become a GREAT Call Center Manager" is a compilation of solutions, strategies and essays, focusing on the special areas that impacts all call center management. The primary objective? To create renewed performance standards, culture and results in the call center. The secondary objective? To help managers in all levels of an organization to become better motivators, better trainers, outstanding coaches, and to improve employee relationships in the thriving call center environment. Management does not need to be perfect. This book, over and over again, emphasizes that management, and its staff, are made up of people who, of course, will never be perfect. What is important is that management be able to oil the parts, fine tune the works, and shine it all up for the showroom.

Your job in using this book is to understand the *human engineering* side of call center supervision. For those who've read my other management training book, "Building Call Center Culture," you'll benefit from this new volume. Included here are many of my favorite thoughts on the subject of call center management, the tricks of the trade. Written specifically for managers, supervisors, agents, trainers, team leaders and executives.

"How to Become a GREAT Call Center Manager" highlights the skills and operational responsibilities necessary to be an effective call center manager. More importantly, it's what you need to know to be better than ninety-nine percent of call center managers today.

Call Center management is more than training, supervision, coaching and leadership. Those are the basic foundations. What you do within those foundations drives results in the call center. How you use ideas to execute the programs herein makes you, and your call center, best in class and best in performance.

I encourage you to view the call center as a series of opportunities and challenges.

Together, we'll identify the characteristics of your center which need tweaking and apply performance development programs to impact its success. We'll focus on the little nooks and crannies of the discipline you won't learn elsewhere.

The call center is a division of two invaluable resources – people and technology. While technology gets most of the attention in today's fast-moving, always changing society, and the call center is certainly in step with if not ahead of the times, it's really people who drive the center. And people need human contact, personal attention – your personal attention. Your mentoring, your nurturing, and your effective leadership. I call this *human engineering*. The call center needs your *human engineering*. No technology can replace the memorable touches that can come only from people.

"How to Become a GREAT Call Center Manager" was written for you, the call center manager, team leader, supervisor, trainer and executive. Enjoy the thoughts. Employ the strategies. Mix and match. And let me know what you think.

My professional services, training and management development firm, CallCenterToday.com, focuses on the *human engineering* of management, people and performance. Contact me anytime. 888-835-5326. Or, DanCoen@ CallCenterToday.com. Or, visit my web site at www.CallCenterToday.com.

It's About Your People –
Your Operations – Your Challenges
– Your Management – Your Culture

Take a moment to reflect on your career, your skill sets, the careers and skill sets of your management team, and the overall operating foundation of your call center. Identify your objectives going forward in call center management, and in particular, the human engineering of the call center.

Describe your position in the call center – how you arrived there – why you enjoy your job – what challenges lay ahead for you within your job.

_____

_____

_____

_____

_____

_____

_____

What type of environment do you work in? Sales or customer care? Help Desk? Inbound, email or outbound? What are the key obstacles going forward in your business?

_____

_____

_____

_____

_____

_____

_____

Describe your culture. What does your company and management team do to drive culture and people and blend people with technology?

_____

_____

_____

_____

_____

_____

Describe your goals in reading this book. Be clear and concise.

_____

_____

_____

_____

_____

_____

_____

What does the word "performance" mean in your call center? How does your call center measure and manage "performance"?

_____

_____

_____

_____

_____

_____

How do the people in your call center view your management team? How do the people in your call center view the call center operation? What are your agents, team and staffs main areas of concern in your call center?

_____

_____

_____

_____

_____

What role does training play in your organization?

_____

_____

_____

_____

_____

_____

_____

_____

1

Remember, Every Day is a New Beginning – It's Time to Motivate Your Agents

Each day is the start of something new in your call center. Build a welcoming environment. Play some games. Teach. Motivate your agents.

Remember, a new day brings new ideas, and new opportunities for success. Get your staff together, grab a white board, and get the creative juices flowing. Your agents and the people they interact with will be happy you did.

▲   Ask your agents for input about the physical look and feel of your contact center. It's their workspace, and they might as well be comfortable. Agents know what helps stimulate their focus. They know what motivates them to do their best. Perhaps they'll ask for pictures, posters, windows, a fresh paint job, even new lighting. Better elevator music perhaps. Do what

Money motivates, even when it's not real! Put executives' faces in the middle of a dollar bill, in place of George Washington or Abraham Lincoln.

you can for your staff now, and put the rest in the drawer for future use.

▲ Present each agent with a personalized nameplate. Engrave the company and department name along with the agent's on the plate. Professional sports teams are on the ball with this idea. They show a personal touch by placing a shiny engraved nameplate right on chairs of their season ticket holders, with a nice surcharge tacked onto the cost of the duckets, of course.

The technique works in the call center too. It gives agents ownership value. Let them decorate the plate to brand it as their own. In fact, management can make each plate a gift to an agent, or distribute them to agents to mark their anniversaries with the company. The power of the gift works wonders.

▲ Put together a department talent show. Group agents into teams and have them coordinate a show, which might take place at the end of the company's quarter. Base the show on themes relevant to your business. Have fun with the event; make it as real as possible, with food, judges and costumes.

▲ Money motivates, even when it's not real! Distribute play money for good deeds, and prepare a reimbursement system for prizes. Use the fake dough to reward a particularly good customer interaction, a quality report, an extra effort, and for agents who work overtime to accomplish an assignment. Have the management team design currency that represents the passion and environment which

Each day brings **new ideas,** and **new opportunities** for success. Get your staff together, get the creative juices flowing.

embodies your contact center. Put executives' mugs in the middle of a bill in place of George Washington, Benjamin Franklin or Abraham Lincoln. Your agents will love it.

▲ Create a team game. Hide gifts around the call center. Provide weekly clues as to what the gift might be and where it could be stashed. Of course, clues can be earned based on performance, or, instead of giving out clues each week your management team can surprise agents with pop-quizzes. Those who excel get a clue. Make the prizes worth hunting for. And play a game consistently, at least quarterly and preferably, once a month.

▲ Establish a department newsletter. Include a featured article, birthday and anniversary news, upcoming events, product training, pictures and feedback about your business. Make the newsletter simple or glamorous, it doesn't matter. What does matter is that it is produced consistently, and is both informative and entertaining. A department newsletter is a terrific way to communicate with your agents and impart important information. Use your department Intranet to post past and present newsletters, and both hardcopy and email methods for distribution.

A department **newsletter** is a terrific way to communicate with your agents and impart important information.

▲ Host once-a-month roundtable sessions with your agents. Invite them to communicate their thoughts. Ask for feedback on any issue they'd like to address. Communicate new product information and industry news. Use handouts.

▲ Display the employee suggestion box you've always meant to put out but never got around to, and make sure your agents know where to find it.

Here's an out-of-the-box idea: Allow agents the opportunity to email suggestions and feedback anonymously from a general email address set up for exactly that purpose, and available from any terminal. That way, agent-management feedback is increased in a simple, user-friendly manner, and the old-fashioned suggestion box goes the way of the, well, the old-fashioned suggestion box.

▲ Subscribe to two or three magazines that influence your business. There are hundreds of trade journals and consumer magazines covering topics which can help your agents shine. Place the magazines in an easy-to-find part of the call center. Distribute photocopies of key articles at meetings and at the start of a workday. Highlight important information.

Every new day opens up a wealth of possibilities for your agents and your contact center. Each day allows your business to build on past successes. All employees want a fun and motivational approach to work. Give it to them. Think creatively. The whole day is in front of you.

The CallCenterToday.com Key Message

Have fun, be creative, take the workplace to another level. Be the best creator and imagineer you can be. Don't let your ideas ever wane...

What inspiration's live in your call center? What steps can you and your management teams introduce to drive creative ideas in your center? List your ideas and share them with the rest of your peers.

_____

_____

_____

_____

_____

_____

_____

_____

_____

_____

_____

_____

_____

Understanding the Five "P's" To Facilitating Feedback

2

Building effective communication and feedback programs in the call center are the ultimate tasks for a call center manager. Ask questions, use answers to motivate, and construct channels of communication that employees actually use.

Managers who recognize the right techniques to building feedback, and those who understand the relationship between human nature and their agents, are well on their way to success. Those managers perceive under which circumstances certain agents will open up and communicate. They visualize circumstances in which the more reluctant agents will participate. Through this recognition, effective management builds feedback opportunities to meet the needs of every class of agents. Feedback programs work best when agents want them to work, and are compelled to contribute.

The agents most eager to provide feedback don't always have the most to say. They petition to talk with

Building effective communication and feedback in the call center is the ultimate task for a call center manager.

management just to be seen, and may have little to contribute. They may feel lonely or ignored, and want to communicate primarily for face time with management. Imagine a feedback room filled with these "needy" agents, each one fighting for attention. How much feedback can be garnered and analyzed this way? How constructive would a meeting like this be? Is this the only feedback management should be gathering?

Conversely, those less interested in communicating may have plenty to contribute, but don't see the channels to do so. The expected quality of and the opportunity to provide feedback should not be determined by the willingness to do so. Some agents choose to communicate only when exceedingly motivated. You may have a few quiet agents who keep to themselves until given an opportunity to share their thoughts. Isn't it funny how some of the best ideas come from agents least eager to join in?

Preparing for Feedback:

Here are some questions to ask:

▲ Might a group of introverted agents provide a successful group discussion?

▲ Should feedback be initiated with agents who don't appear willing to provide it?

▲ Do we want a mixture of participants who are eager and those hesitant to provide feedback?

I believe that an agent's human nature generally falls into one or more of five categories, which I call the *Five P's*. By identifying these categories, management can begin the process of creating superb feedback opportunities in the contact center.

The Five P's to Creating Feedback

1. Possession.

Those agents who want to feel like they can be accountable for what happens in the work environment fall into the *possession* mode. Agents who feel possessive about the call center environment see it as a place to make a difference. It's always a good thing to have employees who feel they "own" their job and their responsibilities – that's also very hard to find. All centers have a percentage of "possession" agents who treat each decision as if it is directed at them, and will impact them personally. Possession agents often provide feedback when presented the opportunity.

> Isn't it funny how some of the **best ideas** come from agents least eager to join in?

2. Prominence.

Agents who feel that consistent communication will move them to the head of the class fall into the *prominence* mode. Not all agents are happy just to do their jobs. They want to impress their superiors, gain upward mobility and new career opportunities. Agents who attempt to create clubs and work late to finish assignments are often agents who thrive on the prominence they receive for doing so. Constant recognition and thank you messages from management drive prominence-oriented agents to continue to provide feedback.

3. Peer Pressure.

Those agents who provide feedback to their supervisors often do so because of peer pressure. The call center is as full of *peer pressure* as high school used to be. Some agents communicate to their supervisors because they want to impact their work environment and their peers. Others are encouraged by their peers to request a conference with supervisors to communicate something that impacts the group. Peer Pressure communication is one of the most common reasons agents request meetings with supervisors. They speak not just for themselves, but for the team around them.

4. Personal Improvement.

Personal Improvement is the primary reason agents seek to contribute feedback. These agents communicate to benefit their own standings. If an agent complains about commission plans, salary structures, data campaigns, talk time percentages, or any other contact center issue, the motivation behind it is likely *personal improvement*. Agents hope to benefit from what is enacted. They're looking for more money, a bigger raise. They want to ensure the safety of their position.

5. Personal (Family) Life.

Finally, when the goal is to benefit their own standings, agents look out for their *personal (Family) life*. Two important parts, the call center or extended work family, and of course, the loved ones at home.

Simply put, most of us work to support our life away from work. It would be great if we worked two days a week and enjoyed our personal life the other five, but in most industries, it just doesn't happen. Family life is a master motivator. The life both at work and at home drive actions, and by extension, results. Motivate your agents by touching on both areas. Combine the two. For example, send letters HOME that congratulate an agent's performance at WORK. Invite an agent's home family to experience his life at the office. Consider the obvious. If both life at work and at home are master motivators, use them to your advantage!

When management acknowledges the *Five P's*, they recognize the human side of their agents. Management begins the process of understanding why their agents communicate. They initiate the process of facilitating feedback. By creating a communications culture which encourages feedback, management builds a better call center environment.

Excellent communication is the key to success in the call center environment. Gain positive feedback by understanding and involving your agents. Use the five P's to create winning opportunities for your team.

How do you and your management team involve your agents in feedback opportunities? List specific feedback programs that your call center embraces. Identify areas that can improve, and, how you intend on improving.

_____

_____

_____

_____

_____

_____

_____

_____

_____

_____

_____

_____

Foundations to the Call Center

The call center is today, and has always been, a place of people. When management understands the human initiative, and creates a roadmap that stresses performance through people, both the organization, and their customers, win.

Below are seven foundations to the call center. Under each, write your opinion and analysis of how your call center performs. Is your call center stellar at a particular foundation? Poor? Do you need assistance in certain areas? Explain.

▲   People

_____

_____

_____

_____

_____

_____

_____

_____

_____

_____

▲ Performance Measurements

_____

_____

_____

_____

_____

▲ Supervisor Accountability

_____

_____

_____

_____

_____

_____

_____

▲ Training

_____

_____

_____

_____

_____

_____

_____

_____

▲   Hiring / Retention / Career Pathing /
     Performance Enhancement Programs

_____

_____

_____

_____

_____

_____

_____

▲   Ongoing Training

_____

_____

_____

_____

_____

_____

_____

_____

_____

_____

▲   Motivation

_____

_____

_____

_____

_____

_____

_____

3

How
Compensation
Upheaval Impacts
Your Employees

Every contact center goes through "compensation upheaval." When this occurs senior management must focus on what's best for the organization as a whole, even if it means overriding the current wishes of frontline management and agents.

This may include changing compensation agreements, overhauling pay scales, or cutting the workforce. The proactive attempts by all levels of management and agents to build  *corporate culture within the contact center suffer a jolt as management must, for a myriad of reasons, implement "compensation upheaval."*

A softening of the economy may only enhance the need for senior management to make decisions that impact their employees' wallets. Instituting a new compensation agreement is one of the great emotional challenges for senior management and agents alike. The wrong agreement can destroy an entire corporate culture. One ill-conceived plan can lead to another, and another still. In a matter of months, these changes can take the steam right out of the company.

Agents may become distrustful, working with less passion for the job, and simply lose their focus.

Instituting a new **compensation agreement** is one of the great emotional challenges for senior management.

Senior management must see that a compensation plan is more than just a set of numbers which determine pay. It's an emotional pact between management and agent. It shapes a culture, identifies the values of a corporation, bonds relationships, and maintains the foundation for future success of the call center. "Compensation upheaval" makes for a huge change. From one plan to the next, agents must modify their mindset and personal goals to meet new objectives.

Reacting to change is difficult under normal circumstances; change in pay accentuates agents' concerns. If the compensation plan penalizes agents in comparison to what they had before, it's seen as retribution, and turmoil ensues. Agents want answers, and need some reason to perform at peak efficiency when their rewards have been diminished. They want explanations for the new plan, and an idea of how long it will remain in effect. The truth is, senior management almost never changes compensation plans to give agents *more* money, and agents know it.

Today's **softening economy** may enhance the need for senior management to make decisions that impact their employees' wallets.

Designing a new compensation plan is a tricky and dangerous proposition. It involves playing with emotions and instituting change. These are combustible elements that can destroy corporate culture. To get the most out of a decision to institute compensation upheaval, management should follow three guidelines:

1) **Recognize that the bond between management and agent is made with trust. The greater the confusion about pay, the lesser the trust will be.**

Employees feel entitled to show a lack of commitment when management flip-flops. In such cases, staff suffers a loss of confidence in superiors, resulting in higher turnover and reduced performance. When senior management prods its supervisors and staff to complete a compensation plan quickly, the urgency communicated often overrides the importance of developing a successful plan which would have maintained the bond of trust.

2) **Design a compensation agreement based on measured objectives and zero discrepancies.**

Too often, senior management pays employees based on one objective, later discovering another more critical to business success. Also, senior management often creates "compensation upheaval" without building solid rules of operation to support the agreement, inundating agents with concerns as loopholes become accentuated. An agreement which leaves a doubt about measurement or objectives is bound to falter because the agents will fail to understand its benefits.

3) Institute the compensation agreement in a way that embraces and enhances the corporate culture.

There is little that's more important to a contact center than its corporate culture. Even in the midst of "compensation upheaval," the culture can be expanded and improved. A change in compensation plans provides senior management with an opportunity to bridge the gap of trust and demonstrate how the move will benefit agents in the future. There are few opportunities to make statements through actions, yet "compensation upheaval" provides that very opportunity.

The line between building effective and misguided compensation agreement is thin. Management must do what is best for the business, but in so doing should present the change in a way that demonstrates a continuation in the building of a sound and productive corporate culture, worthy of their employees' loyalty and trust.

A change in compensation agreements or a cutting of the workforce doesn't have to be the end of the world. Not if accompanied by the right actions. Before any change, however, attempt to make it a structured, well-organized change.

Your agents are motivated by compensation, but it isn't the only motivation. List other motivations that help your team to perform. Have you had compensation problems in the past? If so, what has happened? Where does your call center stand today in its compensation program? How has your organization gone wrong in past compensation programs?

_____

_____

_____

_____

_____

_____

_____

_____

_____

_____

How
New Agents
View
Customer Contact
Technologies

4

Call center managers agree on the great challenges of new-hire training. New agents see dozens of fresh faces, are thrown into a company structure foreign to them, face a unique new program, and are trained on strange computer equipment.

The agents are expected to grasp an organization's culture while immersing themselves in the daily politics and routines of the office. At the same time, they're getting to know co-workers and making new friends. The agent must learn the company's policies and procedures, tackle sales and communications training related to the program, and get used to the work hours of the job. It's a challenging task, and if the agent fails in even one or two aspects of the job, he'll be set back in his quest to increase earnings, and to achieve success and comfort long-term.

More Lessons to Learn

A new challenge has developed recently for agents in initial training. The Internet, intranets and web-based customer contact applications have joined computer-telephone integration (CTI), turning the call center into a tech-oriented environment, geared toward serving customers over various media. This means new learning curves.

New agents often start their job concerned more about the position's technological requirements and less about their communication and product responsibilities.

Because agents continually interact with computers, dialing systems and evolving technology, they start their new job concerned more about the position's technological requirements and less about their communication and product responsibilities. The first questions out of an agent's mouth generally are "How do I use the computer? What type of computer programs do I use? Do I need to learn a dialing system or database program? Can you tell me about the technology and how to use it?"

I estimate that 85 % of my new hires have been intimidated by the computer and various aspects of technology both before and during their first weeks on the job. I feel very strongly about how damaging this is to their initial training.

What Agents Should Learn

Managers should see that mastering technology becomes the agent's smallest concern. Agents should focus on the core aspects of the job first, the tech stuff second. Ahead of technology, areas to emphasize should be:

85 percent of my **new hires** are intimidated by the computer both before and during their first weeks on the job.

▲   The agent's learning the characteristics of the product.

▲   Get the agent ready to successfully communicate with customers and sell the product via the telephone.

▲   Make sure the agent has the potential to become a well-rounded, positive employee.

▲   The agent's contribution to the well being and success of the call center or department.

▲   The agent's understanding of the standards he's expected to meet.

First and foremost, managers should emphasize the importance of everything in the call center environment that's not tech-related. They should focus on turning their new hires into enthusiastic team players and steady individual performers, intent on becoming the best they can be at what they do.

In sales and customer service environments, goals include meeting and exceeding minimum production expectations, improving selling and communication programs, improving call center culture though new ideas and actions, establishing solid relationships with peers, and helping the department

Managers should see that **mastering technology** becomes the agent's *smallest* concern.

and company attain core objectives through excellent work habits and accountable performance.

New agents eventually learn the computer system technology they work with. It may take a couple of days or perhaps months, but with the nature and requirements of their positions being what they are, agents become proficient, and often expert, with the various predictive dialers, automatic call distributor (ACD) set-ups and computer databases as they must.

The common mistake in new hire training is having agents spend so much time focused on perfecting their tech skills that they lag behind in grasping the true skills necessary for success in the field.

When I present a new hire training program, I explore extensively the challenges of technology first because I want new agents to recognize the thought patterns and fears that relate specifically to them. I direct the agents away from their fear of technology and assure them that technology exists to help them in their daily jobs.

I remind agents that technology is a learned skill. I stress that if management wanted technically proficient agents, they would have hired from the IT or MIS departments instead of focusing on those with people skills. I tell them that agents typically fret over the challenges of technology, while failing to learn the programs at hand.

After I've explained the technological basics to my agents and provided them with a reference manual regarding the tools, I encourage them to concentrate on the more important aspects of the job, the customer service and sales aspects of the job.

All managers should spend some time on the first day of training reviewing and summarizing the technology to be used in the call center environment. Failing to do so is to leave agents in a state of paralysis. However, managers must never lose sight of the skills that actually lead to success on the telephone. Those skills are what the call center agents were hired for in the first place.

The CallCenterToday.com Key Message

Remember, it's about people, not technology. The agent should focus on the customer first, the company second, and the computer last.

Describe your new hire training program as it relates to technology training. In your opinion, is too much emphasis placed on the technology and not the sales, script, competition and customer? If so, what changes can you make?

_____

_____

_____

_____

_____

_____

_____

_____

_____

_____

_____

Development of New Hire Training

Your new hire training program should begin well before the new hire agents arrive for work. Development and implementation may take time to strategize, and then implement. However, by planning your new hire training ahead of time, your organization will do it well the first time.

Below are foundations to new hire training. After each, write your opinion and analysis of how you can introduce these programs to your call center. Be creative, and outline steps you and your team can take to execute on designing a best practices new hire training program.

▲ Design a new hire training day by day, hour by hour. Every minute needs to be accounted for. Not just the topics — but what is delivered under each topic.

_____

_____

_____

_____

_____

▲ Prepare a new hire training manual for the instructor and for the students. The instructor manual should outline word-for-word what needs to be delivered. ANY manager should be able to step-in and deliver new hire training.

_____

_____

_____

_____

_____

▲ Divide the new hire training into the following categories:

- New hire orientation

- Product training

- Communications training

- Sales and/or customer care training

- Computer training

- Industry training

- Policies and procedures training

- Competitor training

- Goal setting, expectations and responsibilities training

_____

_____

_____

_____

_____

▲   Create a training calendar of one-minute training
    programs, and deliver these ongoing training
    programs to all students on a consistent basis.

_____

_____

_____

_____

▲   Prepare a strategy for new hire training after the
    classroom portion is completed and the agents
    have reached the floor.

_____

_____

_____

_____

▲   Create training quizzes to be delivered at the start
    of each training class.

_____

_____

_____

▲ Create detailed job descriptions for every trainer in the training department to ensure time management is conducted at a best-practice level.

▲ Create a weekly report that the trainers must turn into their manager, outlining their completed assignments, successes and failures for the week.

▲ Create a weekly planner that the trainers must turn into their manager, outlining the go-forward programs and objectives for the upcoming week.

_____

_____

_____

_____

_____

▲ Prepare graduation certificates for completed classes.

_____

_____

_____

_____

▲ Allow the training department a small monthly budget for motivation, prizes, etc.

_____

_____

_____

_____

5

Philosophies
for Hiring
Call Center
Managers

For a senior executive looking to grow the management staff of his call center, there's nothing that sinks a ship faster than employing the wrong leaders. You need managers that can hit the ground running and impact the performance of agents quickly. The hiring decision is critical and has lasting ramifications. Unsuccessful management hires today lead to failing new hires tomorrow. Bringing in the wrong managers not only puts your supervision behind; it causes setbacks with your agents as well.

What to look for when Hiring Management

Hire an experienced manager? Promote from within the organization? Facilitate fresh ideas from the outside? These are some of the many questions that senior executives must consider. But the key to hiring mangers is not all that complicated a procedure. You don't have to answer a ton of questions and ponder a multitude of issues.

Find managers that can hit the ground running.

Not at all. Instead, senior executives must simply analyze the level of each candidate's *desire* in order to identify the best fit for the organization. *Desire* is the one trait that separates world-class management from the pedestrian. A manager's *desire* to meet goals, his *willingness* to take the extra step on behalf of agents, and his *passion* for out-of-the-box thinking and creating special training programs to increase productivity are what leads to success. The differences between candidate A and candidate B may on the surface be quite slim, but deep down one candidate has the greater *motivation* to see the call center as much more than just a place to work. That's the person you need to hire.

In particular, there are five important traits that executives should review before selecting candidates to manage a contact center:

1. Managers must see the center as a place of creativity.

If your candidate sees the contact center as just another department within the organization, then he may not be the right fit. The contact center thrives on people and emotions to accomplish goals. A leader who understands this is one who can take the center to the next level.

2. Managers must look to accept responsibility for the team's performance.

There are several individuals in the call center who may be responsible for performance. Recruiters, trainers, team leads, agents, etc. But only one person has the true responsibility. If management fails to recognize that "the buck stops here," then that philosophy will trickle down to each level of performer, and a mentality based on the "it's not my fault" mantra will stunt your center's growth.

3. Managers must see the value of communication and feedback in the operating culture.

The right manager recognizes the importance of open communication. Permanent and creative channels that agents are comfortable with and that encourage open feedback build a powerful environment. I've consulted with organizations who host "town hall" meetings several times a year, and others that don't. The difference is clear. The simple gesture of holding a town hall meeting, and dozens of others like it, create a culture of feedback that employees cherish.

4. Managers must view the team of agents as a participatory element to the entire organization.

Talented call center managers know that IDEAS growth comes from out-of-the-box thinking.

They must feel that employees come first, and that peers, outside departments and extracurricular activities come second. Management which gets the value of its employees in relation to the big picture fosters a smooth operating department. It must make a priority of focusing upon the department first, while dealing with other objectives and assignments at another time. The way in which a senior manager prioritizes his goals forecasts the type of manager that individual will be.

5. Managers must search for answers.

Talented call center managers know that growth comes from out-of-the-box thinking. Doing the same thing the same way each time breeds the same results. Your leader must not hesitate to draw upon peers, and seek assistance from other departments to assist in the creation of center's culture.

One **candidate** has the greater motivation to see the call center as much more than just a place to work. That's the person to hire.

Hundreds of critical decisions are made daily in the contact center. Each decision starts with management. Your primary objective in hiring senior managers is to hire the person who shows desire, values *creativity,* promotes *communication,* and has the passion and *willingness* to build a great culture. Once these traits are discovered, the rest falls into place.

The CallCenterToday.com Key Message

Look for four traits in your management candidates: creativity, desire, motivation and willingness.

Your best employees are not always the best managers. What type of management hiring program have you established for your call center? What parameters do you rely on to judge management skills? List the five required skill sets for a call center manager in your environment.

_____

_____

_____

_____

_____

_____

_____

_____

_____

_____

_____

_____

10 Mistakes
To Avoid
In Training
Agents and
Staff

The training process is the beginning of a relationship between management and its representatives. Management must understand the power of quality training. New representatives base their first impressions of their jobs, and decide whether they can succeed, on the basis of expectations set within new hire training. Long-Term representatives predicate their continued success and future prospects primarily on the residual training provided. Training is the support to a quality department.

What starts out as management training *given to* representatives becomes management training *received by* representatives. In other words, management always designs training based on what *they* want to accomplish and when they want to deliver information to their representatives. Management often fails to recognize that training is all about the representatives and what they see and hear and perceive throughout the training. Planning the training class before it begins is a small first step toward alleviating the mistakes so often made. Recognizing that representatives gain knowledge is the *key objective.* Trainers must view their training from their students' perspective rather than from their own perspective.

Training may be segmented into various stages. *New Hire Training* is the most important training program, because representatives who don't understand the product, corporate objectives, or key aspects of communicating fail to do their jobs well. New Hire Training is the time where management has the opportunity to gain their representatives' trust, or to lose that trust. *Residual Training* is essentially a downplayed aspect of training. Many supervisors believe that once they have trained representatives, those employees can sink or swim on their own. They forget that ongoing training sharpens skills. Small one-on-one sessions, group workshops and E-learning seminars should be mixed together to foster a clear training methodology.

Training is the backbone to the call center. It's often times forgotten, slightly focused upon and considered an expense.

Training is also segmented within a call center operation. There is computer training, product training, residual training and competitor training. Each piece is critical to performance. The following is a primer for the 10 mistakes management should avoid when training representatives:

1) Don't Assume Your Representatives Understand What You Understand.

Don't assume your representatives understand the relationship between telephone, product, customer and company. These four segments bring success or failure to organizations. The telephone is a channel of communication between the company and the caller. The product is the area around which telephone conversation revolves. The customer is the central point–customers initiate calls and require assistance. The company is the backbone that provides the representatives with credibility. You know this. Your representatives may or may not know this. Explain it to them.

Training is all about the employee and what they see, hear and perceive.

2) Ensure Representatives Understand They Represent Your Brand.

Management makes a critical training mistake when they fail to see their representatives as the communicators of their corporate brand. Who has more interaction with customers, the CEO or the plethora of representatives that receive E-mails and telephone calls from customers on a daily basis? Representatives present the corporate brand to an audience of customers, and this is the audience that matters most. Training must impart to representatives *what* the corporate brand is, *how* it was developed, *why* it exists and *where* the company is going because of it. Most importantly, the corporate brand must express to customers why it benefits them most. When representatives can't articulate their corporate brand, the corporate brand becomes meaningless.

3) Instill A Sense Of Company Culture Into Training.

If representatives successfully believe in the corporate brand, then they also need to believe in the company's corporate culture. Culture provides the motivation and desire. Representatives will work an extra hour, stay on the telephone an extra minute, and help their peers complete projects all because the corporate culture encourages them to do so. When representatives believe in the company culture they express that belief to customers. They do just a little more because leadership has trained them to do so. It makes all the difference.

4) Involve Representatives In All Facets Of The Company.

Because representatives embody a critical channel between company and customer, it is important that they understand the full breadth of the corporation. Many times representatives feel they have a sense of the company, but they don't understand the sales, marketing, business development and internal departments that form the backbone of the business. Make no mistake about it: only representatives who understand the company as a whole can help set the expectations of their customers. The actions of sales and marketing oftentimes form customer perceptions, and it is the job of representatives to handle these customer perceptions. In a vacuum, representatives may find this challenging. Yet, when they understand what each level of the company does, they will not only find their jobs challenging but will achieve greater success.

New Hire Training is extremely valuable. It needs to be outlined and organized. Ongoing training is essentially forgotten in the mix.

5) Be Certain To Teach Representatives How To Use Technology.

In the old days, training representatives involved training them with regard to the product. Within the past 15 years, technology has become an equally prevalent training challenge. Oftentimes management fails to recognize how representatives are impacted by the technology they are required to use. Technology has become the "hidden dragon" for representatives. Representatives are many times so afraid of computers, dialing systems and technology as a whole that they spend all their time either avoiding it entirely, or worrying about it too much. Management will make a gigantic blunder if they fail to provide a thorough training program to their representatives. Representatives that gain insight about technology can move on to more relevant topics such as product knowledge and communication techniques. But until representatives are comfortable with technology, it will always be a harbinger hanging over their head.

6) Train Representatives On What and How They Will Be Judged.

Management is so focused on getting the job done well that they sometimes forget to tell their representatives exactly what they will be judged on. Then, they forget to show them. Representatives emerge from training with general ideas on what their objectives are, but less of an idea of what will earn them praise, awards, raises and a promotion. Training sessions fail to define what allows a representative success within the corporate structure. Management also often forgets to show the representatives exactly how judging occurs. In the call center venue, monitoring of phone calls or auditing of records may involve the use of forms. What are those forms? What requirements are listed on those forms? When do those forms get issued to the representative? In a vast majority of instances, representatives work to improve themselves and their standing at work. Therefore, representatives need to understand what they will be judged upon, when they will be judged, and how the judging will affect them.

7) Ensure That Residual Training Is Implemented After New Hire Training.

There are **several blocks** of training, each deserving its own program. Computer training, product training, ongoing training, communication training, sales training, new hire training, training on teamwork.

A common perception is that training begins and ends once the new hire training period is completed. This is where management loses their representatives. By not receiving consistent and detailed residual training sessions, representatives gain neither the skill sets nor the confidence to improve at any level other than the practical day-to-day work level. Management should institute classroom training followed by on-the-floor training, followed by residual classroom and residual on-the-floor training, for an endless period of time for each employee regardless of experience. It is important to recognize that training does not stop after the new hire leaves the classroom. That is when training begins.

8) Don't Train Representatives On Everything In The Beginning.

Training representatives can become a balancing act. Do the representatives need to know everything about what they do, or just enough to get the job done? Quality training begins with the understanding that too much information clutters. By cluttering, the valuable information fails to take precedence. Therefore, management should train their representatives on the most important ten to thirty percent of the information first. Focus on training representatives on everything they need to know to get the job done, not everything they might want to know. The "want" can be presented later during critical residual training sessions. For instance, perhaps initial training can be divided between the most important and less important topics regarding product knowledge, customer communications and product information. After the representatives have gone through this initial training and worked as part of the team, they can then receive less important yet valuable training on product knowledge, customer communications and product information. What management will find is that after giving representatives the most important ten to thirty percent, representatives will work on their own through their daily applications to discover much of the remaining seventy to ninety percent.

9) Teach Representatives How To Communicate With Customers.

Representatives are the first and most powerful communications channel with customers. Therefore, management must be careful to design a training program that introduces the basic and advanced elements of telephone and customer communications. Many times management designs a training platform that presents the facts, questions and answers, without introducing the communications training necessary to teach representatives how to articulate these facts, questions and answers to the customer. Failure to train representatives on the "how" leaves a big gap in training. Customer communications includes traits such as:

–   Listening to the customer

–   Identifying what the customer wants

–   Conversing with the customer so the customer has confidence in the representative and the company

–   Providing the customer with feedback that gets the customer to an end-result they will be pleased with

10) Dedicate A Training Person To Lead The Process.

Would you be stunned to learn that many call center departments don't have one dedicated trainer that conducts or oversees training? Instead, they delegate training to a supervisor who has other duties, a manager who may not be prepared to conduct training and therefore delivers a poor class, or a part-time trainer who also serves as a representative or team-lead. An organization that takes pride in its call center must ensure they have the budget for a training organization. The key mistake many organizations make is treating training as the low-rung and least important part of the organization. This is because management doesn't see immediate revenue payoff from the training department. The irony is that training is predominately responsible for facilitating the success of representatives. How representatives view their company, their brand, their corporate goals and the value they place in their customers defines the success and failure of a company. Training must be a key priority for the company to achieve success in the long run.

The CallCenterToday.com Key Message

Training is a critical part of the call center curriculum. However, classroom training differs from training on the main floor. Both are prerequisites for success.

Identify the strengths and weakness of your present training program. Can you develop a better program? If so, what would you do? Is your call center management team picking up training where the training department leaves off? If not, describe ways to change behavior.

_____

_____

_____

_____

_____

_____

_____

_____

_____

_____

_____

_____

7

Implement Benefits of a
Top-notch
Communication Culture

Creating and implementing top-notch communication culture is one of the great challenges facing call center executives worldwide. The absence of a communication culture in the center is a recurring problem for these organizations. It attacks every aspect of management and agent performance.

Imagine communication culture as the overriding tenet of philosophies and practices that forms the foundation for everything that happens in the call center. It encompasses the structure of managing agents and supervisors on a daily basis, affects sales and customer service performance, creates opportunities for feedback and growth, and helps overcome roadblocks which invariably arise on an hourly, daily, and weekly basis. Call Center culture begins and functions through communication.

There is no question that every call center, by nature, has some form of communication culture. Often, it's not what management envisions. Or perhaps it's the culture they want but not the one they truly need. All levels of management must recognize that a

> **Train your senses to be as attuned to communication culture as they are to food, body language, music and visuals.**

communication culture of some type exists in the call center today. The objective is to turn that communication culture into a world-class dynamic.

While most call center managers understand the reasons for agents' under-performance and design concepts to optimize opportunities, they don't always have the time, energy or ability to bring these concepts to fruition.

Every call center has an element of a communication culture. It may resemble the culture of a prison, a bank, a basketball arena, or even seem a bit like Disneyland. As you walk on your floor today, you should get a sense of the type of communication culture your center has now. You can train your senses to be as attuned to communication culture as they are to food, body language, music and visuals. While each call center embodies some form of communication culture, they're not all top-notch in nature. Our job is to explain why.

The challenges of creating world-class communication culture are daunting. Many managers view their time and call center operational issues as too important to change or create a fantastic communication culture from scratch. Many executives are of the opinion that "Since we're making money and things are sailing along, it ain't broke, so to speak, so let's not fix it." They're wrong.

With a philosophy like that, you can imagine the type of culture that exists in the call center. Yuck! Let's keep in mind, the main challenge in building a top-notch communication culture is to assure that it's all about people.

The principles mentioned above involve human emotions, human thoughts, human conflicts and human feelings. They present opportunities and team challenges that management and staff may simply not be qualified to initiate. Consequently, even if executives are inclined to implement a new and powerful communication culture, they may have difficulty getting buy-in from management and staff.

Concepts for making communication culture happen may be digested and manipulated in different ways by different people. Building consensus is tricky. If five parties want to try something nine different ways, how can an accord be reached?

Many Executives think that "Since we're making money and sailing along, it ain't broke, so let's not fix it." They're wrong.

Why create a new communication culture for agents? Perhaps creating opportunities for one agent is a doable process, but doing so for a large group of agents is a too much to ponder. Why create such a daunting task for managers when if may not work? And what about

It's **simple.** Develop great communication channels and you'll improve performance, and set records.

the challenges when it comes to buy-in?

Creating a communication culture is a two-way street. Each of the principles mentioned above invites agents to contribute to building a communication culture. The process simply will not work without agent participation. Asking one or two agents to take initiative outside their daily telephone job is a doable process, but asking multiple agents to do so opens up issues.

It's a well-known fact that when something involves the interaction of many people, challenges abound. That's why one-on-one basketball is easier to play than five-on-five, for example, and why small crowds are easier to contain than large ones. It's no surprise then that agents wonder why they should invest their time and energy for a call center. Making agreements, carrying out duties and developing correct courses of actions can paralyze call centers and render any attempt to build communication culture moot if the participants don't agree to bind together. The objective of creating a new communication culture forces all staff to think about binding together. Management immediately takes a step back and asks, "Will our call center be able to make the leap?"

Management must view the call center as more than just a place to do business. In our society, many corporations see their business as a place for employees to come and go, with the simple goal of doing their job well and getting paid for it.

Few center managers see the full potential of their workplace. A world of creativity is automatically built into the call center business. The environment, from the seats lined up in a row to managers on the floor motivating, is extremely conducive to inventiveness. Agents working the telephone in the office make for a captive audience. Management must be creative to keep motivation at a peak.

That said, it's important to build a communication culture with bells and whistles. Use games, banners and sirens, yes literally, sirens! Playing cards, signs and clanging bells are appropriate forms of communication in the call center. Agents often get restless glued to the telephone, and benefit from management that takes steps to address the repetition and the general difficulties of the daily regimen.

Agents seek attention and acknowledgement that their hard work is being noticed. Give them contests, awards, prizes and surprises. They're a more creative and articulate group than are other type of employees. The call center has a built-in opportunity for communication culture. Like the agents, management must think creatively to maximize performance.

With a compassionate communication culture, executives can make their call center a Super Bowl of operations. They can turn daily operations into daily stories. Management must make the commitment to perform above and beyond the norm. They must see the potential to boost performance objectives, and to jump-start agent opportunities.

When managers understand that performance is cultivated through *superior communication channels* which involve agents and their opinions, the agents will set records for you. It's that simple. Develop and implement great communication channels and you'll improve performance. Channels may include team meetings, one-on-ones, newsletters, voicemail, email, letters and the like. Agents will exceed goals in every measurable area when management does its all to establish a *culture in the call center that emphasizes agent input and opportunities.*

Yes, creating communication culture takes work, and yes, it can be complicated. And no, it doesn't occur in a day. But when completed, it'll change the results and environment of your entire call center for years to come. Building a strategic communication culture is *that* important.

Go to great lengths to create positive communications channels. Pull out all the stops, be creative, and make it about people.

Have you had experience in other call centers? If so, what made those cultures different from your present culture? How did they utilize communication channels to their advantage? List your communication channels and their impact on you team? What should you do differently to use communication channels?

_____

_____

_____

_____

_____

_____

_____

_____

_____

_____

_____

_____

Call Center Management and Operations
Assessment

1. How does your management team administer operations on a daily basis?

_____

_____

_____

_____

2. How does the work environment affect your call center agents?

_____

_____

_____

_____

3. Who are the management leaders that establish and implement strong communication channels on behalf of your agents? Do they separate themselves from other management personnel? And if so, why?

_____

_____

_____

4. What aspects of your call center would you call world-class? Describe what is special about each one.

_____

_____

_____

_____

5. Which areas of your center afford agents clear opportunities to participate?

_____

_____

_____

_____

6. What steps can be taken to promote communication between agents and management?

_____

_____

_____

_____

_____

7. How would you rank management in terms of the following:

   • Coaching agents.

   _____

   _____

   _____

   _____

   _____

   • Listening to agents.

   _____

   _____

   _____

   _____

   _____

   • Encouraging feedback from agents.

   _____

   _____

   _____

   _____

   _____

- Developing skill sets of agents.

_____

_____

_____

_____

_____

_____

8. How often do agents participate in decisions?

_____

_____

_____

_____

_____

9. When was the last time your call center attempted to build a new culture? What was the result?

_____

_____

_____

_____

8

The
Call Center Battle:
People vs. Technology

Senior management faces constant challenges in the development of corporate culture. A battle brews between making technology the overriding arch in creating corporate culture versus developing an employee-centric approach that encourages a people-first mentality.

I've spent hours with call center management who base their business plans on creating top software and technology, seeking to meet bottom line budgets and appeal to customer demands, leaving the human element aside. I have spent an equal amount of time with management who direct most of their budgets toward people, management and training in an effort to achieve customer satisfaction. In both cases, senior management is on the right page. In neither scenario is an effective balance in place.

Senior management must identify the role their people play in concert with technology. Perhaps your center has put in place a series of technological improvements. The upgrades are designed to increase customer satisfaction, improve employee performance, and even improve the level of communication and culture within your operation. Balance is imperative; without it the people side of building a communication culture may be lost.

Senior management must identify the role their people play in concert with technology.

The entire organizational focus becomes geared toward software and technology, while performance dwindles and retention decreases. I was part of a recent technological overhaul that went south. I watched the excitement in introducing new technology become quashed by employees who misunderstand its benefits. Performance actually decreased after the new technology was introduced. Nobody felt comfortable using it. It's buying a car without first getting a driver's license. The features are great, the opportunities are limitless, but nobody has the motivation or ability to use the technology. Consequently, the features never serve their purpose.

Upgrades in technology, from CTI to CRM to web-based interaction are introduced to help business achieve better performance. But managers need to take a step back and ask themselves, has the overriding approach to technology blunted the company's ability to service customers? Has the brilliant technology within the center slowed the company's performance because elements of the technology are being under-utilized and are in fact interfering with customer service?

Your call center will fail if performance hinges squarely on the shoulders of technology, rather than with the people who use it. With the freedom technology brings, corporations tend to believe that technology alone will make the works run. Senior management forgets it's the people who utilize the technology.

Management can get the most out of its investment in technology by following some guidelines which ensure an equitable balance between people and technology:

1.) If you're going to invest in the technology, use all of it.

Many call centers have dozens of technology-based platforms not in use by management and supervisors. It's either because employees choose not to use it, or because they simply don't know how to. An investment in ACD, predictive dialers, CRM packages, and web-based platforms have no meaning in your customer-centric environment unless you provide training in its usage and importance.

Technology alone won't do. It's the people who use the technology that matter.

2) Remember, technology is a beginning, not an end.

A former manager of a national call center described to me how cyclical senior management's approach has become. First, call centers focused on their people, with training, management and motivation. Then they focused on software and Internet applications. Soon after that, once again people became the central focus. Call centers today are once more leaning more heavily on software than ever before. A consistent balance is what's needed.

3) Build a corporation that treats each customer as an individual.

Many new software packages improve the corporation's assistance to customers but fail to provide a mechanism for measuring success. When customers go "one-on-one" with employees, the real test of the company begins. Are agents trained to help the customer? Are they ready to use the new technology, and competent enough to quickly and ably assist customers?

The balance between training agents and management to deal with customers and training them to utilize applied technology is critical. If you've implemented an array of new software and made sure your people know how to use it (and how to function without it for that matter,) your customers will be the beneficiaries. Once accomplished, you've come a long way toward creating a sound technology-based operation which your people can make flourish.

People first, technology second. Take care of your employees, who will in turn care for the customer. And, understand how to use your technology.

In your opinion, how much of your technology sits wasted and never used? What training programs are in place to provide ongoing technical support to your agents and management team? How can you help make your technology a useful application in the call center?

_____

_____

_____

_____

_____

_____

_____

_____

_____

_____

_____

_____

9

A Daily Game Plan

Does your call center have a daily introductory game plan? If you think there's something amiss about the beginning of the day, guess what, there is.

If your center is without a solid plan to keep your agents motivated and focused, then you're just not doing everything you can do to promote performance and retention.

Here's an example. I once consulted with a call center where 250 agents began their day at 6:30 in the morning. As I would stroll the center floor at the start of the shift, I would see four supervisors huddled in an office, two in the breakroom, 45 agents on the telephone actually working, 78 late or not on the premises, another 100 agents in the breakroom or restrooms, and a whopping two supervisors hard at work on the floor.

The source of the problem is easy to find. In the scenario described above, management started the day off with as bad an example as you can imagine, and the agents followed suit. It starts at the top, doesn't it?

Imagine a restaurant where you seat yourself and the waiter fails to serve you, or a self-serve buffet that's completely devoid of food of any kind. What about an airplane full of passengers with the pilots hanging out in the lounge?

If you think there's something **amiss** about the beginning of the day, guess what, there is.

The leadership communicated to call center agents in the first 30 minutes of the day sets the stage for the whole day. The best boss I ever had started every day by walking into my office with a rousing welcome. He knew that if I felt good about what I was doing, my agents would feel that way too. He understood that if he got me off to an upbeat start, I'd transfer my enthusiasm to the agents.

When the guy stopped his positive start to my day for whatever reason, I noticed my own motivating of the agents drop off accordingly. He fell into bad habits and as a result, so did I. And so did my agents.

Whether you have seven agents or 700, whatever the size of your center, always remember that fresh start. The initial 30 minutes of the day are absolutely critical.

They say breakfast is the most important meal of the day. And those first 30 minutes at work are the most important 30 of the day. Start it off right.

What is the management daily plan in your call center? If none exists, brainstorm a daily plan now and introduce it to your management team. Do you have a daily game plan?

_____

_____

_____

_____

_____

_____

_____

_____

_____

_____

_____

_____

_____

10

Revitalize
Workplace
Culture...EARLY!

I'm always impressed by call center supervisors who understand the importance of managing and inspiring agents. The development of a center evolves around creating a place of momentum, ingenuity and inspiration. Supervisors and agents should seek to create a better sense of environment in order to be successful.

Although motivating, communicating and developing plans to inspire agents can be an enjoyable aspect of the job for both parties, it's difficult for supervisors to keep agents at a peak, day in and day out. It takes constant effort to supervise eight to fifteen agents, much less twenty-five or fifty. In addition to pure management of their agents, supervisors typically have reports to complete, meetings to attend and developing issues to handle. The time available to promote action programs for agents may be limited and requires effective time management.

Yet supervisors who focus on their agents' well being succeed much more often than those who don't. Agents know which supervisors care about them, and which one's don't. A typical call center has so many distractions that it becomes all too easy for supervisors to ignore their primary objective of managing agents in favor of less taxing assignments. If a supervisor takes the easy way out, the agents knows it.

Supervisors who look to move forward with tangible elements of success must remember what goes into the making of a top-notch call center culture. For starters, here are some important principles which define the culture of a call center.

▲ **Condition your agents to expect something the minute they walk in the door.**

Do your agents walk through the door to start the day and then scatter? Let your agents know that you'll present a message to them in the same area of your center each day. Use an overhead projector or

Supervisors and agents should seek to create a **better sense** of environment.

white board, or use an area of the center for a display case with pictures, decorations and messages.

Each morning, have your supervisor guide the agents to the main spot in that part of the room. The objective is to display a valuable message that your employees either want to or need to read each morning. This will condition your agents to gather at the start of the shift in one location. Secondarily, you'll bring each agent to a central venue where you control the message, guaranteeing the communication of important

Bring agents to a central location where you control the message, guaranteeing the communication of important messages to the agents exactly the way you want to.

messages to the agents exactly the way you want to. Scatter is eliminated.

▲ **Train agents to accept your objectives.**

Agents believe what you say when they see that what you say matters, and is of value to them. When you present a daily message that informs (and hopefully entertains) and that is to their benefit, subsequent messages will be looked to for value. Just a few messages at a time, mind you, there's no sense bombarding the agents with too much all at once. Just focus on one or two important directives, things that need to be shared now.

▲ **Make it a point of communicating with each agent daily.**

Regardless of the size of your center, it's crucial to communicate with agents individually each day. Agents look for opportunities to communicate with management in non-telephone settings. Here are some ways to get some personal contact.

1. Say "hello" to each agent. Ask them how they're doing?

2. Send a voicemail to each agent.

3. Send an email to each agent.

4. Leave a message on the chair of each employee.

5. Leave a personalized note on the desk of each employee.

What you go out of your way to do in three to thirty minutes' time pays dividends in ways unimaginable. Don't be afraid to make contact!

▲ **It pays to motivate. Do so.**

If agents see their supervisor with a vested interest in their success, the parties will share what amounts to a partnership, not a dictatorship. It doesn't happen by itself – motivation leads to vested interest. A quick meeting, a special gift, and in particular a pat on the back are simple yet effective motivational tools that can't be understated. The principle is simple: Supervisors must constantly motivate the agents, not just for the agents' benefit, but for their own.

Outstanding communication culture exists when supervisors work toward building and maintaining an upbeat environment. World-class communication culture starts with the call center supervisor. Agents will gladly accept the motivation the supervisor provides. All you have to do is lead by example.

Get your message out first thing. Keep your agents moving forward with action, motivation and attentiveness.

Does your call center do the same thing, the same way, each time? Are your agents conditioned to perform based on management actions? If not, describe ways, in your environment, to create these programs.

_____

_____

_____

_____

_____

_____

_____

_____

_____

_____

_____

_____

_____

Systems for Great Call Center Management

Great call center managers recognize that systems breed results. The systems your team puts in place will accentuate your strengths. Why be good when you can be great?

Below are systems to call center operations. It's all about call center management. After each, write your opinion and analysis of how you can introduce these programs to your call center. Be creative, and outline steps you and your team can take to execute on designing best practices operations.

▲   Implement consistent daily team meetings between management levels.

_____

_____

_____

▲   Prepare an end of the week report for managers and supervisors. The purpose of the report is to organize operations and assess results. It gets the managers and supervisors to begin driving performance.

_____

_____

_____

▲ Prepare a planning guide for the upcoming week. The purpose of this report is to plan the upcoming management, motivation and training programs.

_____

_____

_____

_____

▲ In a sales environment – teams, competition, consistent touches and emotions are what drive results. Divide your group into as many teams as possible.

_____

_____

_____

_____

▲ Understand that teams need to be advertised and marketed to. Develop a marketing campaign to your employees!

_____

_____

_____

▲   Create detailed job descriptions for every level of management.

_____

_____

_____

_____

▲   Implement a better channel of communication between operations and training as it relates to new information, job duties and meetings. These two departments should work as a group.

_____

_____

_____

_____

▲   Prepare a monthly goal setting program. Hold management accountable to their goals and representatives accountable to theirs.

_____

_____

_____

_____

▲   Create an "account implementation" checklist. This checklist has a listing of every requirement that must be completed to lift a new account off the ground successfully, from hiring the appropriate employees to IT, management responsibilities and training.

_____

_____

_____

_____

▲   Create a communication center in the call center that houses information, such as flyers, posters and products, of your accounts. Use this center as a central meeting place – and – be certain new and existing clients see the communication center as a place you use to promote them as clients.

_____

_____

_____

_____

11

The
Big Deal
About
E-learning

Six months of development and implementation finally lead to an epiphany; your contact center has incorporated E-learning, but your agents, well, that's another story.

Management has introduced the E-learning packages you've bought. For months consistent sales and product training have been conducted via computer and web based channels, yet neither your agents' performance nor the center reports show much growth. The agents see E-learning almost like a break from work, rather than a challenge to improve. You've spent thousands of dollars, and your ROI is, well, didily. Senior management wonders, "What's the big deal about E-learning?"

At this point you might question the selection of the E-learning package. With dozens of models on the market, the goal is to find the E-learning training platform that's customized and relevant to both your agents and business.

There's another possible solution. In fact, it may be quite specific to your call center culture. Maybe your management team left your agents out of the introduction to E-learning process. Or perhaps management skipped the usual, on-the-ground classroom training needed to bookend the E-learning process.

Let Fellow Agents Develop the How of E-Learning

E-learning training is just starting to become a value-added possibility in the business environment. Management is recognizing that just because there's been a buzz generated around E-learning, it doesn't mean that the entire world of corporate culture is going to embrace it, especially after classroom training has been in place for generations.

E-learning training should not be a stand alone "virtual training." It needs to be a well-rounded package. A successful E-learning program works when combined with more traditional forms of training. Examples include customized workbooks, books, tests, and follow-up hardcopy materials. Agents grasp the high-tech world of E-learning when the human element they're so used to is included in the process.

Furthering the E-learning dilemma, contact center agents often fail to acclimate to E-learning because they don't know *how* to benefit from the training. Let's face it, management can spend all its time explaining to agents *why* E-learning is beneficial (i.e. it's high-tech, it's fun, information is displayed easily, blah, blah, blah,) but until they teach their agents *how* E-learning helps, agents won't respond.

The how is critical because it teaches relevancy in real-life situations. Consider this: *Why* does E-learning improve telephone skills? Because it teaches new ways to present company features. *How* does E-learning present ways to improve telephone skills? E-learning is only as powerful as the development of pre-and-post training programs that prepare agents or review for agents what was learned in the e-training course.

You've spent thousands of dollars and your ROI is didily. Senior management wonders, "What's the big deal about E-learning?"

The *how* is the classroom training and follow-up lessons that make E-learning function. The *how* is the repetition. It conveys information after an E-learning training session that invites feedback about the training. E-learning by itself, although relevant, leaves the educational cycle incomplete.

I recommend the development of a powerful traditional classroom training course that serves as an addendum to the E-learning process. And I encourage management to include agents in the building process, before and after the training programs. New platforms of training like E-learning fail when introduced in a vacuum without agent buy-in, usually when agents are unclear about its value.

Agents tend to go with what their peers say. They believe that those responsible for the development of training know something they should know. Agents see their peers as credible conveyers of information, and buy into what's presented more easily when it's presented by them, rather than by management. So your current agents, the employees who have yet to benefit from E-learning, are the ones best suited to develop the training packages which explain *how* E-learning benefits the team.

The contact center is in the unique position of being able to build targeted teams to facilitate training. Agent teams are a staple of contact center culture. Why stop creating agent teams for E-learning simply because it appears to eliminate the human element? Allowing agents to form training teams, and to present their fellow agents with a compendium of materials to support E-learning training, are great ways to condition agents to benefit from E-learning. Here are three examples of agent-driven teams which help make E-learning training a success:

▲ E-learning Team

The E-learning team assigns a variety of upcoming training projects to another group of specialized agents, whose job it is to create pre and post-training programs. Comprised of both managers and agents, the team serves in an oversight capacity.

▲ Product Training Team

Two or three agents in the center are designated "go-to-agents." Prior to an E-learning class, the assigned agents develop a short training program showing the others how best to benefit from the upcoming E-learning product training. These agents then follow-up the E-learning training with a prepared question and answer program to fill in gaps formed during the training.

▲ Sales Training Team

Prior to an E-learning sales training session, have the sales training team put together an expectations package describing what the agents should learn during the session. Then instruct the team to design a short quiz for the agents to take afterwards. Build a program of prizes around the E-learning sales training.

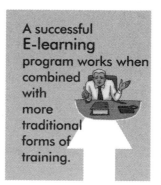

A successful **E-learning** program works when combined with more traditional forms of training.

E-learning is exciting and new and is certainly a training option that's here to stay. But agents must grasp its significance if they are to learn anything from the training. Management can require agents to attend E-learning sessions, and they can design their own on-the-ground classroom programs to complement E-learning training, but for the biggest bang from training, you must involve agents in the process. Training and conditioning agents and the building of a better call center culture comes together best when management involves agents in training one another, especially with E-learning.

Remember, E-learning is a new deal for agents. Let them know it works, it's for their benefit, and will help them to succeed. Your agents won't take it as a given. You shouldn't either.

E-learning is a big deal. When properly combined with traditional training and agent input, it's a surefire tool for success.

Prepare a training process that includes traditional classroom learning blended with E-learning. Would that work in your call center? If not, how can you work around those obstacles? Is E-Learning an option in your call center? Why or why not?

_____

_____

_____

_____

_____

_____

_____

_____

_____

_____

_____

_____

Building Agent/Supervisor **Relationships**

One Question at a Time

12

Call Center managers require specific techniques to help them build relationships with agents. While the center is about performance and technology, it's first and foremost a relationship-oriented entity.

Agents build tenure and perform consistently in part because of the satisfaction they get from their relationships at work. Managers who create excellent working relationships with their agents consistently elicit superior performance and results. When things go well, it's easy to maintain a happy home, so to speak. The effective working relationship between manager and agent is what gets a center over the hump in a challenging situation.

Asking questions is a key component to call center operations that should not be underestimated. Telephone sales and customer service representatives ask questions in affirming the direction of a call, to gain information, and to establish relationships with customers. In like manner and for similar reasons, supervisors and managers ask questions of their sales and service reps. The question-asking technique works

105

for all types of professionals in a myriad of industries. Questions open the relationship-building process, and show a level of interest between people.

In a typical call center, agents question supervisors. That's the norm reinforced by conditioning. Agents question supervisors about product issues, regarding computer problems, and concerning their issues with company policies. Agents look to be a part of the decision-making process, so they ask questions. It keeps them involved.

Managers who create excellent **working relationships** with their agents consistently elicit superior performance and results.

Do supervisors use questions to build relationships and to learn from their agents? My guess is yes, sure, but not often enough. Managers limit their questions because they're making the decisions, and don't make the thoughts of agents a priority in each decision. Asking questions of agents serves a purpose for which management should be cognizant. Not simply to gain information, asking questions helps build relationships for the future, and establishes a positive environment in which the agent-supervisor relationship can flourish.

Take a step back and look at your supervisory team. How often do supervisors actively pose positive, non-threatening questions to their agents? Do they use artful questions to facilitate performance? How often are questions used to establish an open communication forum? Are your supervisors making a genuine effort to reach out to their teams?

Questions open the relationship-building process, and show a level of interest between people.

A whole new agent-supervisor relationship begins when supervisors ask questions of their agents. Here are some ways to do this:

1. Ask Agents Questions To Which You Already Know The Answers.

Use the latest technology and CRM packages to track your agents' progress. For instance, suppose your center measures talk time, pause time, total dials, completed sales or total sales made. Find the excellent performers who are performing above the norm and deserve recognition. Go to them and say "Hey, how's your day going today?" Depending on the response, you might say "I see you did XYZ today. Way to go." The key is to be encouraging. Show interest. Get them talking about themselves. Listen.

2. Ask Open-Ended Questions To Discover What Agents Need.

Open-ended questions are general questions designed to elicit information. The questioner doesn't know what the response is going to be.

Simple, unexpected, open-ended questions can be a relief to agents. This is especially true when agents could use a minute away from the phone and computer.

Sometimes the least complicated questions elicit the best conversations, and facilitate a tremendous call-center culture. Questions such as the following make a difference: "How are you today? What's new with the customers and prospects today? How did you do so well yesterday? Did you get the XYZ issue resolved? Can I do anything to help?" These questions, while simple and logical, are rarely communicated from manager to agent. It's imperative that managers demonstrate their interest in the agents' day-to-day challenges.

3. Ask Questions To Establish Value.

Imagine working in an environment where your boss really doesn't care about what you do or what you think. Sad, but it happens. By simply questioning agents, management is able to demonstrate that the agents are a valued part of the organization. All agents want to believe that their supervisor values them. By asking questions, supervisors provide agents with the opportunity to comment, create, propose strategize, and communicate issues important to them. Your questions provide the agents with an outlet and a culture they value.

I've spent thousands of days walking up one aisle and down the next, stopping at selected cubicles merely to let agents know I care about their performance and want to help them do their jobs. Some agents want to focus on work and don't have the energy to talk, while others need to focus on work. In those cases, I just let them do their thing. The vast majority of agents, however, appreciate the opportunity to share what's on their minds.

Whatever responses you get, the important thing is that you have asked the questions, and made a personal connection. Remember, questions open up platforms for opportunity. Issues a manager visualizes present one type of challenge, while issues that a manager can't see, those root problems that fester under the surface, present even greater challenges. Questions bring those hidden items out into the open. Discovery, one question at a time, can be a great relationship builder for agents and managers.

Keep those lines of communication open by showing interest in your people. Engage the agents with genuine questions and listen to the responses.

A key to telephone communication is "question-answer". That is also a key to call center management. Do you and your management team engage the agents in human interaction? Do you show you care? If so, describe those efforts and how to continue to make them better. If not, outline how your management practices can change.

_____

_____

_____

_____

_____

_____

_____

_____

_____

_____

WHY ASK QUESTIONS?

Asking questions encourages interactions between agents and supervisors.
Asking questions creates a cheerful and creative atmosphere.
Asking questions establishes a culture of openness and interaction.
Asking questions makes the culture a place of value.
Asking questions conditions agents to understand that management cares about their thoughts.

Tips to Creating a People Oriented Culture

Below are tips to the *human engineering* of your call center. Under each, write your opinion and analysis of how your call center performs. Is your call center stellar at a particular foundation? Poor? Do you need assistance in certain areas? Explain.

▲   Keep Agents on the Telephone

_____

_____

_____

_____

_____

_____

▲   Bring Motivation to Each Agent in Simple Ways

_____

_____

_____

_____

_____

_____

▲ Train

_____

_____

_____

_____

_____

▲ Make Goals Simple

_____

_____

_____

_____

_____

▲ Make Compensation Simple

_____

_____

_____

_____

▲ Promote Flexibility

_____

_____

_____

_____

_____

▲ Be Organized

_____

_____

_____

_____

_____

▲ Manage by Using Technology

_____

_____

_____

_____

_____

New Recruits

13

Need Your Attention – Train Rookies to Reach the Majors

In baseball, successful organizations devote vast resources of time and money developing up and coming prospects to ensure a constant flow of ready and able talent to the big club. The minor leagues were formed and are maintained today for the express purpose of preparing fresh players for a higher level of experience.

The contact center is kind of like baseball. Each week or month, your company must hire and train new agents to guarantee a continuance of top performance. Unfortunately, supervisors are so focused on meeting core goals and reacting to whatever comes up during the day, that they often neglect their responsibility to provide new agents with the detailed, hands-on training they need to be successful. They're not alone – it happens in baseball too.

I've noticed that after new agents are smothered with supervisor attention for their first 5 to 10 working days, they're often all but forgotten. I call this "The Build Them Up and Ship Them Out" style of managing. Supervisors provide a bit of training, show the agent the ropes, and

Supervisors are so focused on **reacting** to whatever comes up during the day, that they often neglect their responsibility to provide new agents with constant, detailed, hands-on training.

say "Good luck, let me know if you need anything." The irony is palatable at best.

Supervisors need their agents to do well yet can't focus on all of their agents all of the time. The result more often than not is that the supervisors end up losing track of their new agents. Later, if the agents underachieve, supervisors seek to orchestrate a performance development plan to help the agent get up to speed before inevitably being forced to take real action. But supervisors have the tendency to implement these plans *after* new agents have demonstrated they're not meeting minimum objectives, rather than *before*, when new agents need the training most. It's seen generally, that the initial new agent training once started in earnest ends up being a trickle down form of the intended training, at best.

Let's look at three reasons for supervisor falloff of continuous training of new agents, and some solutions for each:

Situation: Supervisors are busy working with veteran agents. Veterans produce 90-95 % of what's needed, and do the most to assure that the company and departmental goals are met, so it's natural for supervisors to work with them. During initial training, the supervisor focuses on his new group, but just until the newcomers reach the call center floor. At that point, they're pretty much left to their own devices.

Solution: Keep the new agents in a central location. This allows the supervisor easy access to all new hires. Also, new agents often create a bond with one another through their shared experience. Bonding gets them to rely upon one another for answers, problem solving and motivation.

Situation: Supervisors tend to forget new agents even exist sometimes because with newness comes agent trepidation and perhaps a bit too much silence. New agents are sensitive to "getting along" with their supervisors, and when they have issues and concerns, they're often hesitant to speak up at all, or they go to a peer for assistance. The supervisor is generally the last person the new agent contacts with any questions they might have.

The initial **new agent training** once started in earnest ends up being at best trickle down from the intended training.

Solution: Meet with new agents daily for three to five minutes. Ask questions, search for opportunities to coach and encourage feedback. Make sure the new agents feel confident they can come to management without losing their supervisors' confidence. Design a residual training program that covers one or more topics each day in these few minutes.

Situation: New agents are often intimidated. Since new agents don't know the ins-and-outs of the company, they're more likely to suffer with a problem than to ask for assistance.

Solution: Pair each new agent with a veteran agent. Give the veteran flexibility in his job while assisting the new agent.

New agents are a pipeline to the future. Without a quality training program that encourages performance, the pipeline dries up and business loses its edge. New hire training begins with initial classroom training, but must encompass on-the-floor residual training and classroom refresher training. There is a process and a purpose to quality new hire training. Be constantly thinking about your new agents. They are the future.

Follow up with initial new agent training. See to their success with a nurturing approach that makes them feel a part of your winning team.

Divide your call center agents into different categories. Spend 60% of your time with the struggling 20%. Try to build from the bottom-up. Spend time with all your agents, but particularly those that you invested time in training. Strategize ways your management team can review each agent as an individual and then design a training program tailored to each of their needs. Don't let your training department do all of the training. Take charge.

_____

_____

_____

_____

_____

_____

_____

_____

_____

_____

14

Executive Considerations For E-learning

Smart senior executives know the formula. Training plus knowledge equals success. They're in tune with the concept that solid break-in training coupled with outstanding residual follow-up benefits everyone involved with the organization. Customers, prospects, new and veteran personnel alike. Everyone benefits, all of the time.

Today's execs must answer two basic questions. First, what kind of training program(s) do you need? Second, what's the best way to incorporate the newest channel of training – E-learning?

Choosing a quality training program for your staff is a challenge. It's an important decision, and you can't be too careful. Customer Relationship Management (CRM) has taken the business world by storm, opening opportunities in the E-learning spectrum. In spite of advancements in CRM introducing E-learning to businesses, it's still common for senior executives to contact professional trainers to design and present traditional in-person training programs, rather than go the high-tech E-learning route. Execs and students have been conditioned to believe that in-classroom training is the first way to convey and receive information, and such conditioning is difficult to overcome.

Meanwhile, a battle is taking shape. Dozens of E-learning companies are positioning themselves as leading facilitators of training to businesses. They're using CRM as a vehicle to present their outstanding technology. E-learning types see their product as much more than a tool for engineers, technicians and computer programmers, or for the college campuses that first embraced the interactive medium.

Smart **Senior Executives** know the formula. Training plus knowledge equals success.

They know E-learning is here to stay, and that it's a dynamic option for companies to use. E-learning corporations proudly portray their engaging, interactive training packages, powerful visual programs and outstanding streaming media as "real life" training. Yet, for whatever reason, some senior call center managers remain skeptical. Managers want simple, cost-effective training at a good margin. They see the potential of E-learning, sort of, but wonder if their organization can implement the right CRM infrastructure required for effective E-learning.

And most importantly, senior management can't help but come back to the thought that whichever route they take, whether it's traditional or E-learning training, they need results. Consistent, dependable results. They don't know if the world is ready for E-learning training only, and it's something they keep coming back to.

The answers to E-learning lie with CRM, which makes E-learning thrive. The phrase CRM was coined a few years ago primarily to define the stunning growth of technology in the customer contact center. The technology was intended to facilitate a positive relationship between business and consumer.

But what does CRM really mean to the executive trying to understand E-learning? How does CRM relate to E-learning? Have you noticed that for every commentary about the wonders of CRM, there's another crazy explanation for it?

Here are my two cents worth: I define CRM as *"a scaleable strategy that allows customers, prospects, employees and businesses to share in multiple communication platforms, in order to increase the effectiveness of business."*

In essence, CRM involves a multitude of channels of communication, from tech-based software through Internet-oriented platforms, all designed to effectuate opportunities in business. Channels include training between employees and management, interaction between staff and customers, and communication between company and prospects. In turn, CRM has spun off E-learning.

The E-Learning Option

E-learning works only in tandem with right thinking. Howard Nehdar, an industry thought-leader, says it best. "There is no question that E-learning works, and many call center executives have utilized it to train their staff and their customers. However, our goal is not only to provide call centers with what they need, but to condition call center executives to recognize that what they need is E-learning. There is still some skepticism that E-learning can do the trick."

> Call Centers need **customized training,** live interaction betweeen students and instructors, and a pro to facilitate the training.

The skepticism involves the perception that the cost of the technology needed, and the development required, may outweigh the benefits of the programs. Sure, the thinking goes, benefits of E-learning, like reducing travel costs and delivery time, and reaching a large audience all from a simple setting have their value. But at the same time, these features help little without results. So the thinking goes.

Call center execs had much the same concerns with new systems just years ago, when they were afraid of CRM, CTI (Call Telephony Integration,) computer networks and predictive dialing systems. Only the early adopters forecasted and reaped the benefits of bringing in those systems from the get-go. Today, they're in almost every contact center.

In the traditional model, E-learning consists of four critical components which work together to assure success for a corporation: Internet based video, integrated media, easy-to-use content management, and reliable delivery. These four components are the foundation of a powerful E-learning platform – and with this foundation successful E-learning corporations build training that works for their clients.

Imagine your staff in a conference room, preparing to sit in front of a big-screen monitor for an extended period of time. The screen comes alive with a solid training program when the four components are put together correctly. That's really just the beginning.

Call Centers need customized training, live interaction between students and instructors, and a pro to facilitate the training. These value-added features provide executives with the quality training – and the better results – that they mandate for their staff. Most of the top E-learning firms are more than capable of meeting these goals, but it comes at a price. You just need to decide if the price of being an early acceptor of E-learning is worth the training investment for your staff.

What Call Center Executives should look for in E-Learning

In recent years, corporations have started customizing their E-learning programs specifically to meet the demands of executives. "Many customers are skeptical because they're not sure what's available and how to implement it," explains Shereen Fogel, a leading assessment and evaluation specialist.

"They're confused about what courses are applicable to their business, and whether the courses tie-in to the training they need." Fogel believes that in the past, E-learning companies seemed to think that their main competition was the other guy out there selling E-learning solutions alongside them. Not so. It was really the traditional methods of training they were up against.

It was the traditional methods of training that customers were conditioned to use, the ones customers actually *liked* using. They already understood its process and its value, and quite simply, they knew it worked. So hotshot E-learning programs ended up less effective because they weren't customized directly to the customer. They didn't take into account what the customer valued most.

The fact that some E-learning companies created phenomenal software was tempered by the fact that they couldn't get their customers to use it. It was either too advanced or simply inappropriate to the needs of the customer.

Today, the thriving E-learning company understands that the usefulness of a quality product begins with the client's ability to find value in it. E-learning companies are attempting to simplify communications and education for their clients. For instance, top executives have communicated to E-learning vendors that content must be a primary factor, and that students recall great visual images.

When E-learning companies give their customers what they want, they're successful. The companies are beginning to understand that accessible content and engaging platforms are only relevant if they're adaptable to changing business conditions. A "canned" software package will only go so far. The training must constantly evolve with the account, and the E-learning company must consistently be part of its clients' growth.

What executives should evaluate when selecting an E-Learning vendor

With dozens of credible E-learning firms presenting their benefits to clients, senior executives have a host of decisions to make. Assuming management has a desire to use E-learning as a training solution, management must weigh the strengths of each company carefully. Some have strengths in technical media, while others provide customized soft training in fields such as human resources, accounting and desktop word programs. For those deciding on an E-learning solution, I advise management to identify the following:

> **E-learning companies now understand that accessible content and engaging platforms are only relevant if they're adaptable to changing business conditions.**

▲   An E-learning partner must provide the client with specific content, design and tech support. Creating an E-learning program that incorporates the company brand is a priority, and customization of the package is a must. E-learning packages lacking the tech infrastructure to meet customized goals can bring a training session to a grinding halt. A qualified vendor should provide value-added enhancements such as publishing tools, viewership reports and 24/7 customer service.

▲ An E-learning platform must incorporate people-to-people interaction. Chat between individuals across multiple locations, one-on-one conversations between students, video-based slides, and professional facilitators to manage the training session are basics to the training.

▲ The staff must be conditioned to understand the values and potential pitfalls of E-learning, which simply cannot work if your staff isn't behind it. They must believe in the process of learning, while interacting and communicating their training ideals with that of an E-learning platform.

▲ E-learning needs to be combined with in-house training. Don't give up on the traditional methods of training. E-learning can't overcome the intimacy of teacher / class integration, nor can E-learning perform every function that customized in-house training can supply. Both are necessary. Make sure the E-learning vendor agrees.

▲ Executives should avoid a one-shot deal with E-learning. Ongoing use is highly recommended. Stick with it. The best E-learning programs are those that have multiple sessions enabling conditioning to occur. Presenting a two-hour session and deciding from that one session if a particular method of training is proper for the contact center is not the way to go. It's not fair to either the employees or the E-learning vendor. It takes time for students to adjust to something new, and E-learning is no exception.

▲ Have staff members provide feedback on the presentation. Ask them about the format, as well as the content of the presentation. Get plenty of input. You may want to collect feedback through written or verbal exams, or by simply passing out feedback forms about the E-learning. Either way works.

▲ Get proof of financial stability from the E-learning vendor. As E-learning companies come-and-go, management must be cognizant of the financial stability of their new partner. Few E-learning companies have long track records. Their ability to stick around, establish relationships with your people, and build upon emerging technologies is critical for your company.

Don't rush in selecting an E-learning vendor, and, don't give up after selecting an E-learning program. Patience is the key.

Has your organization embraced E-learning? If not, how would you go about marketing an E-learning program to senior management in your call center? Do you believe in the value of E-learning as a regular component to your training?

_____

_____

_____

_____

_____

_____

_____

_____

_____

_____

_____

_____

_____

How Can Companies Use E-learning?

New Hire Training	Sales Training
Residual Product Training	Computer Training
Customer Demonstrations	Internal Cross-Department Training
Company-Wide Conferences	Motivational Program
Introduce New Marketing Programs To In-House Staff And Vendors	Customer Reinforcement Program To Introduce Value-Added Resources
Product Launches	On-Site Trade Show Presentations
News Conferences	Customer Service Training

15

Solutions on the
human engineering
of your call center

45 Quick Tips to Guide Call Center Performance

1. Work diligently to build constructive relationships with your peers, with others in management, and with all departments in your organization. Departments include human resources, technical support, IT, marketing, outside field sales, etc. Your ability to develop excellent relationships pays dividends. When your agents need assistance, be available.

2. Supervisors often underestimate the value of maintaining relationships with employees outside the call center. While they may recognize the value in doing so, they may not take the time required. It's critical for supervisors to take the initiative to build effective relationships away from the center.

3. Make a consistent effort to employ motivational contests and incentive programs. Don't concern yourself so much with the pomp and circumstance

or size of the program – that's not important. Just keep motivating.

4. Use posters, pictures, fliers and drawings and whatever promotions you can think of to hype up the contests. Keep your agents updated with results, so they know where they stand through the program. The key is to continue on a daily, weekly and monthly basis, to present these motivational programs. Make them a common occurrence. Such programs emphasize performance, goal setting, and striving for objectives. Don't forget to think "outside the box" for ideas.

5. Introduce wild prizes, wacky gifts, inexpensive goodies, whatever you can come up with.

6. Giveaways serve as a wonderful motivational experience for agents. Don't consider just the expensive, overpriced items to be valuable. Cash is great, but there are other things you can do. The best prizes are often the simple, inexpensive, and fun stuff. Don't be shy about going to the 99 cents store and buying 65 wacky gifts for a total of $50.00. Use a grab bag to deliver contest prizes. Create gift certificates and coupons on the computer. Give them out for special performance. The bottom line is, creative prizes motivate agents too. It's not the price of the item that delivers the message.

7. Make *your* work environment *the* best place to be in the company.

8. Agents who stay become expert at their jobs over time. Minimal turnover saves the company money on hiring and training. In some companies, the call center is a place to begin a career, and exit for greener pastures. There may be no denying that better money can be made elsewhere, but employees who have worked in bad environments, and for poor supervisors, value a "family friendly" department almost as much as a 10-15% raise. It's acceptable to lose an employee to a higher salary or a greater opportunity. Just make sure that when all things are equal, your call center culture is the best, and makes the difference in retaining the agent.

9. Be demanding...of yourself.

10. Performance starts with management. I've seen many supervisors who expected all-star performances from their employees, but didn't demand it of themselves. Delegating down is old school management. In a call center, the supervisor is the guy who should arrive first and leave last. He's the one who should always be thinking of improving culture and performance. Working hard and smart isn't a badge of honor. It's just good management to do so. Supervisors need not outlast one another at the end of a day to see who leaves work last. That's silly. But supervisors should get there before their agents and have the center set-up properly prior to the shift. And, barring excused circumstances, the supervisor should rarely be the first person out the door at the end of the day. When

the supervisor demands of himself, his leadership stands out.

11. Condition agents through repetition.

12. Employees perform well when conditioned to do so. They also perform well when they do the same things over and over. Perhaps we all can recall the conditioning through repetition experience in grade school and junior high. Same classes day after day, same seats, same teachers. Over and over with the same subjects, break times, friends and enemies, the same start and end of day times. We were conditioned as students based on repetition, and most of us performed at an acceptable level. Run your center along the same lines. With consistent occurrences come consistent actions.

13. Use the Internet to find and distribute articles on relevant topics, not-so-relevant topics, interesting topics, cultural topics, competition-based topics, etc.

14. Agents respond to supervisors who look for opportunities to engage agents in topics not readily associated with their job. You can always print and distribute articles to agents when they walk through the door, in the middle or end of the day. It's easy enough, and makes for yet another opportunity for agents to learn to communicate better with customers and prospects, all because management gave them the tools to do so.

15. Use voicemail, email, "chat" and tech-based applications to communicate messages.

16. Expect the call center to look differently as time passes. New technology increases the chances management has to communicate messages. In the old days, it was either team communication or individual communication. Computers and copiers have allowed mass production of fliers, newsletters and written messages. Today, most centers have voicemail, email, chat, and web-based chat to facilitate communication. While an agent is talking to a prospect, for example, the supervisor can be listening at his desk, send a quick message to the agent, and have the agent instantaneously read and communicate the content to the prospect. Many centers allow the supervisor to voice the message to an agent in much the same manner, producing the same result. This is just the beginning, and management must take advantage.

17. Completely remove the phrase "I don't have enough time" from your speech.

18. If you don't have time to do the right things, does that mean you only have time to do the wrong things? Most call center managers think they only have time to do "X" amount of work. Wrong. Prioritizing the work from right to wrong is key. Most call center supervisors also think their duties are more complicated than the rest. Wrong again. Ace managers rise to the occasion. They know that it's when things turn sour that it's hardest to find

the time and energy to do great things. When you pass on something important because of perceived time insufficiencies, you miss the chance to do what your reps need you to do.

19. Be at work 30 minutes before your agents.

20. Imagine a restaurant where your table is bussed and prepped 30 minutes after you arrive. Agents should be at work thirty minutes before a shift, but rarely are. Supervisors should arrive thirty minutes before a shift to plan their day's activities. Do so for your representatives, not for yourself. If you're not prepared to help your reps when you get to work, then how can they expect their needs met, their questions answered? If you only have time to churn out a quick motivational program rather than a good one, what's the point? If you're rushed, disconcerted and disorganized, how can you demand the best from your staffers?

21. Document, document, document! Make a record of everything that happens each day.

22. Document things for educational purposes. Each time an agent closes a sale, makes a good presentation or achieves superior customer satisfaction, a summary of the event should be recorded in a supervisor's notebook. When an employee is counseled regarding an issue, same thing. Write down the person's name, the date and time, and a brief summary of the discussion. Every counseling session, each award given, every event that can be used to motivate and teach an agent in

the future should be documented. Supervisors also learn from this practice, and become better man agers in the process. When you refer to your notebook to see that you spoke with "Larry" 22 times in a particular month, for example, it's safe to say that "Larry" knows it too. When a supervisor acknowledges something like that, an agent sees how dedicated the supervisor is to his success.

23. Be consistent.

24. Greet agents when they walk through the door. Have a note or a flier or a message for them at a regular place and time.

25. Never assume that your training department has truly trained your agents. Do it yourself.

26. Your training department may do an outstanding job training your agents, but it's your success, not theirs, that matters to the boss and to the company. Training by trainers covers the how-to. Training by managers covers the how-to-succeed.

27. Provide consistent sales and communications retraining sessions. Provide consistent product knowledge and computer knowledge retraining sessions.

28. Agents on the telephone are your frontline representation. They talk to your entire customer base. Training them once doesn't cut it. Constant retraining provides repetition, which leads to effective conditioning. Send a signal that you *want*

your agents to do well, and you send a signal that you *need* them to do well.

29. Don't feel obligated to make quick decisions when quick decisions are not required.

30. Rarely are management's quick decisions as warranted as they seem at the time. If you took one or two or even three days to really think about an important decision rather than one of the snap variety, would we be surprised to learn that *nothing* was missed because of the extra time allotted? Would we be surprised to see that the "emergency" before you were solved just as well in three day's time, and probably better, because it was thought through carefully? Take your time. Get it right the first time.

31. Don't be afraid of technology. Use it to your advantage. Agents all too often think of technology as a barrier to their communication, when it's really an asset. When management sees technology as an asset, agents do too, and thousands of dollars for useful equipment are put to work. Agents' resistance to technology fades with time. They'll see how it benefits their job, and will embrace it eventually. Provide great training and repetition to motivate your agents to use the technology provided to them. Be patient, but encourage them to get their feet wet, and jump right in.

32. At the end of each day, take a sheet of paper and recap the events. Plan tomorrow's.

33. Organize your priorities and try to perceive what's going on around you. Think of what has just happened in order to prepare for what will happen.

34. Produce weekly and monthly summary reports that have meaning.

35. As much as management may prefer an ever-pretty picture of what's going on in the call center, it needs to hear about *everything*. With today's technology, it's easy to put together accurate appraisals regarding just about anything, from attendance to performance. Do so. Make sure the reports are thorough, get to where they need to go, and are considered. The best reports allow for comment, suggestions and insight. Produce them that way.

36. Take a select group of agents to lunch each month. Ask for their input.

37. Feedback is good for management and agents, and along with a relaxed group lunch comes a solid flow of feedback opportunities. Agents like to spend the company's money, and an award like this provides an outlet for feedback, while at the same time allowing a little grandeur for all individuals.

38. Turn an extra space into a break room, reading room, or game room.

39. It's easy enough to turn an extra room, space or cubicle into its own little world, and worth the effort. Games, food and reading material are inexpensive. More importantly for the business, the

room may become a work arena that breeds culture and ideas which benefit the entire business.

40. Reward agents for meeting a goal each month. They must have a value-added finish line to work toward.

41. When an agent meets a company-sponsored goal, she has accomplished a terrific feat. Make note of the achievement with a public pat on the back, at the very least. Simple acknowledgements may come in a company newsletter; through a verbal presentation at a meeting, prizes; even with a posting of names in a special spot in the office. If you feel meeting a goal is worthy of acknowledgement, your agents will too.

42. Make sure your agents have individual and daily goals to reach

43. Executives can be quite good at planning the monthly, quarterly or long-range goal; agents respond with a shorter destination. Supervisors should be providing agents with daily goals. Sales goals may be two, three or six sales for a particular day, and also counted toward the monthly or quarterly objective. Customer service goals may involve time on the telephone talking, number of spreadsheets completed, etc.

44. Open windows, hang pictures, posters and drawings in your department.

45. Care about doing a great job. Focus on goals. Be accountable.

The Call Center Managers
Action Planning Sheet

The journey, here, is coming to a close. Yet, the journey in your organization is just beginning. Now, the fun part. Use this page to create a work plan for tomorrow, and many tomorrow's, in your call center, inside sales, customer care, help desk or telemarketing organization. Be fluid-don't skimp on either words or ideas. Outline your strategies and implement your plans.

Contact us at 888-835-5326 or MyCallCenter@CallCenterToday.com if you have questions.

1. What programs do you intend on implementing in your organization?

_____

_____

2. How will your magement team be impacted by the new programs?

_____

_____

3. What drawbacks and obstacles do you expect to encounter?

_____

_____

4. What action-steps must you take to ensure these programs are implemented?

_____

_____

_____

5. List the areas of your call center which need improvement.

_____

_____

_____

6. List the areas of your call center which are "best practices".

_____

_____

_____

7. What are your key goals going forward in your orgnization.

_____

_____

_____

_____

Sample Management Development Workshop from CallCenterToday.com

Introduction

A. Navigating in the call center environment

B. Recognizing people-to-people call center management

Understanding the Principals of Call Center Culture

A. Emotions, feedback, creativity, relationships, ownership

B. Defining the supervisor-agent relationship

C. The life of a supervisor, team leader and manager

D. The life of an agent

E. Technology and its relationship to people-to-people management

Simple Tenets of Call Center Management

A. Six principles of call center management

B. Emotions versus Data

C. Listening and Hearing

D. C.A.L.M.

E. Creating a world all its own

Designing a Spectacular Communications Culture

A. Creating the story of your call center

B. How call center agents view the call center

C. Available communication channels

D. Balancing new agents and seasoned agents

E. Concept – Desire – Implementation

Facilitating Feedback Opportunities in the Call Center

A. Technology advancements

B. Group and Individual dynamic

C. The art of questioning

D. Gathering of blab

Building the Supervisor's Job Description

A. Step-by-Step design of the supervisors job description

Building a Culture Away from the Telephone

A. Training, training and more training!

B. Call Center bill of rights

C. Successful compensation agreements

D. Career pathing opportunities

E. Organizational teams

Identifying, and Supervising, through Agent Classification

A. Ranking agents

B. Managing the three tier process

C. 15 area's of agent supervision

Ensuring Supervisor Accountability

A. 25 Programs to the successful call center

B. Implementing performance development programs

C. Creating a quality assurance program

D. Delivering coaching and training

E. New Hire Training

F. Time Management

G. Benchmarking Performance

Call to Action

To schedule a workshop led by Dan Coen please call Toll Free 888-835-5326

or email MyCallCenter@CallCenterToday.com

Sample Telephone Sales Training Workshop from CallCenterToday.com

Introduction

A. The Mindset of Telephone Sales In Today's Society

B. Establishing A Relationship And Building Credibility

C. Creative Selling -The Story-The People-The-Value-The Differentiation

Understanding People-to-People Communication

A. Listening and Hearing

B. Visuals and Verbals

C. Emotions vs. Data

D. Trusting The Telephone Sales Process

E. Themes, Images and Concepts

F. WIFM

G. The Value of needs vs. wants

H. Gain Info / Give Info / Commit

Your Product, Service and Offer has a Story. What is it?

A. The Story Behind The Story

B. Show and Tell

C. Building Emotional Attachment

D. The Needs Of Your Prospects Versus The Needs of The Company

E. TSR / Product / Customer – Who Has The Ball?

F. Sizzle Points That Matter

G. Look To The Future

H. Creating a world all its own

Asking Questions and Conversing like a Friend

A. Ask / Respond / Question

B. Trial Closing

C. Open and Closed Closes

D. Why Ask? Why Not?

E. Directing The Presentation

Building the Telephone Presentation

A. Seven Steps To A Sales Strategy

B. Primary and Secondary Objectives

C. Developing A Story

D. Customer Profiling

E. Personal Goals

F. Structuring The Presentation

G. Purpose – Process – Payoff

Handling Objections and Closing Sales

A.   The Unique Value and Purpose

B.   The View From The Owner

C.   Transition Phrases

D.   Why They Object

E.   10 Key Ways To Handle Objections

Call to Action

To schedule a workshop led by Dan Coen please call Toll Free 888-835-5326 or email MyCallCenter@CallCenterToday.com

Comments – Questions – Feedback

Do you have comments, questions or feedback about this book? Contact CallCenterToday.com. We want to hear your thoughts.

Toll Free 888-835-5326

MyCallCenter@CallCenterToday.com
www.CallCenterToday.com.
PO Box 571533
Tarzana, CA 91357

About Dan Coen

Dan Coen, President of CallCenterToday.com, specializes in the **HUMAN ENGINEERING** of call centers, inside sales, telemarketing, help desk and customer care organizations. He is the author of the books *Building Call Center Culture*, *Friendly Persuasion*, *Inspiring Call Center Performance*, and *Ring up Phone Sales*.

Dan teaches that people maximize results, increase ROI, and build culture. He is the recognized industry leader in driving call center performance and people development through interactive workshops and hands-on consulting. His keynote speeches, seminars and training programs have brought a dynamic, lasting exchange of ideas to business organizations around the world.

Dan began his career on the telephone, in both customer care and telephone sales roles. He supervised agents at a young age, and began developing call center management programs that increased agent performance and management discipline. His first book, *Friendly Persuasion*, tackles telephone sales training. His second book, *Building Call Center Culture* is an industry leader, and examines management's role in operating a call center and supervising its employees.

For more information about Dan Coen's consulting solutions, keynote speaking, workshops and training programs, or to order copies of his books, please call 888-835-5326 or 818-703-1022. Or, contact Dan via email at DanCoen@CallCenterToday.com. Dan's website is located at www.CallCenterToday.com.

About CallCenterToday.com

CallCenterToday.com is a professional services organization that specializes in the **human engineering** of call centers, their managers, trainers, operations and people. What's the secret? Dan Coen, President, said: "The call center is today, and has always been, a place of people. When management understands the *human initiative*, and creates a roadmap that stresses performance through people, both the organization, and their customers, win."

People and technology can turn an every day call center, inside sales, customer care or telemarketing organization into a results-oriented, customer centric profit center. CallCenterToday.com was founded to teach in the knowledge areas of management, operations and training. Dan said: "It's about a system of assessment, information and implementation. What does the manager do each day? What is involved in operating the call center? What steps are required to benchmark performance and measure results? How does the team leader get performance from agents? Why doesn't management use technology more effectively to get better results? Who manages your after-hours call center? How do you build a call center from scratch?"

CallCenterToday.com specializes in some of the following:

▲ Call Center Reorganization

▲ Development of Call Center Management

- ▲ Training Programs for Call Center Management, Agents, Representatives and Trainers

- ▲ Benchmarking Statistics and Measurements

- ▲ Telephone Sales Workshops

- ▲ Hands-on Management of your Call Center

- ▲ Performance Enhancement Programs

- ▲ The Art and Science of Becoming a GREAT Call Center Manager

- ▲ The Human Engineering – Motivation and Culture

- ▲ Save-the Sale, Winback, Cross-Sell Programs

- ▲ Customer Care on the Telephone and Via the Internet

- ▲ Building the Call Center from Scratch, start to finish

- ▲ Hiring and Managing a Service Agency

- ▲ Site Selection and the Look-and-Feel of your Call Center

For more information, contact CallCenterToday.com at 888-835-5326 or 818-703-1022. Or, email MyCallCenter@CallCenterToday.com. Visit the web at www.CallCenterToday.com.

Books For Call Center Management

**Training That Speaks Directly To The People Of The Call Center:
Managers, Trainers, Team Leaders, Executives, and Supervisors.**

**Ideal for Inside Sales, Customer Care,
Help Desk and Call Center Organizations.**

Ring Up Phone Sales   #of copies _____ @ $24.95 ea = Subtotal $ _____
Telephone Sales Training <u>AUDIO</u> Book

Friendly Persuasion   #of copies _____ @ $24.95 ea = Subtotal $ _____
Telephone Sales Training Book

Friendly Persuasion   #of copies _____ @ $16.00 ea = Subtotal $ _____
Telephone Sales Training Workbook

**Inspiring Call Center
Performance**   #of copies _____ @ $24.95 ea = Subtotal $ _____
Call Center Management <u>AUDIO</u> Book

Building Call Center Culture #of copies _____ @ $24.95 ea = Subtotal $ _____
Call Center Management Book

Building Call Center Culture #of copies _____ @ $16.00 ea = Subtotal $ _____
Call Center Management Wookbook

**How to Become a
GREAT Call Center Manager** #of copies _____ @ $24.95 ea = Subtotal $ _____

Order Your Call Center Management Books Today!

Call Direct: 888-835-5326
Fax Order Form To: 818-703-1022
Web Site Ordering: www.CallCenterToday.com
E-Mail Ordering: books@CallCenterToday.com

Mail Order Form and Check or Money Order Payable To:

DCD Publishing
PO Box 571533
Tarzana, CA 91357   USA